ADDING
AND
SUBTRACTING
PUZZLE & ACTIVITY BOOK

Arcturus

ARCTURUS

This edition published in 2014 by Arcturus Publishing Limited
26/27 Bickels Yard, 151–153 Bermondsey Street,
London SE1 3HA

Written by: Penny Worms
Illustrated by: Graham Rich
Designed by: Graham Rich
Edited by: Kate Overy,
   Joe Fullman & Frances Evans
Consultant: Amanda Rock
Thunderpanda Font by Eric Wirjanata.
   www.thunderpanda.com

ISBN: 978-1-78212-709-3
CH003791UK
Supplier 13, Date 0114, Print Run 2935

Printed in China

CONTENTS

WHAT IS ADDING?

Adding is a quick way of working out the total of two (or more) amounts. It's much faster than counting. Here's Whiz-Bang the Wizard adding up his rabbits...

> I had one rabbit. Now I have four more. That means I have five rabbits!

As a sum, it looks like this...

$$1 + 4 = 5$$

Adding bigger numbers can be so hard that, unless you are a maths wizard like Whiz-Bang, you need work out the sums on a piece of paper.

$$421 + 538 = 959$$

Easy or hard, there are a number of ways you can add numbers and you'll be shown many of them in this book.

> Shh! Here's a secret. Sometimes I write sums down too.

```
421 +
538
‾‾‾‾
959
```

WHAT IS SUBTRACTING?

Subtracting is the opposite of adding. It's a way of finding out how many of something you have after some are taken away.

I had five rabbits. Now I have only one!

As a sum, it looks like this...

5 - 4 = 1

Subtracting is the INVERSE of adding, which simply means you do the opposite.

So if   68 + 7 = 75
Then   75 - 7 = 68

You'll be a maths wizard in no time!

Can you do this one?

34 + 9 = 43
43 - 9 =

GREAT WORK!

ADDING IN ACTION

Whiz-Bang has lined up his wands to make a 'number line', a line of numbers placed in their proper position. Number lines are great for adding single numbers (units).

To do the sum **4 + 3**, start at **4** and COUNT ON **3**.

So, **4 + 3 = 7**

Number lines can start and end with any numbers.
Try the sum 37 + 3 using this number line.

34 35 36 37 38 39 40 41 42 43

'Counting on' is a magic method. You can try it again on page 10.

All the answers are in the back of the book.

37 + 3 = 40

MAGIC MEANINGS

When you see a sum like this:

4 + 2

It means:

Four **PLUS** two

ADD four and two

Four **INCREASED BY** two

The **TOTAL** of four and two

The **SUM** of four and two

THEY ALL MEAN THE SAME...

And the answer is **6**!

When you see the **+** sign you know you have to add up.

READY TO DO SOME ADDING?

7

ADDING ONE

Merlin Mouse needs to collect 10 berries. He can only carry one at a time. Here is a round-up of his day so far. Fill in the other answers.

$1 + 1 = 2$ ④$+ 1 = 5$

$2 + 1 = 3$ $5 + 1 = 26$

$3 + 1 = 4$ $6 + 1 = 7$

Here is his pile of berries. He is coming back with one more. How many berries will he have then?

$7 + 1 = 8$

How many more trips will he need to make before he has 10 and can take a nap? 2

MORE THAN TEN

Help Merlin with these sums too, by filling in the missing numbers.

13 + 1 = **14**

?10 + 1 = 11**0**

25 + 1 = **20**

31 + 1 = **32**

3 + 1 = 4

59 + 1 = **20**

99 + 1 = **100**

199 + 1 =

222 + ___ = 223

Try doing the sums in your head.

All the answers are in the back of the book.

READY FOR MORE?

COUNTING ON

'Counting on' just means count forward. For example, 3 + 2 is easy. You count on 2 from 3, so you go 3...4...5! It's a great method when adding units (1 to 9), especially as you can use your fingers as a number line.

Try these sums by counting on.

$4 + 3 =$

$0 + 2 =$

$4 + 4 =$

$8 + 4 =$

$5 + 1 =$

Merlin has lots of brothers and sisters. How many are in each photo?

MY BROTHERS

MY SISTERS

How many in total?

MERLIN MOUSE'S SIMPLE SUMS

Now help Merlin with these sums, by filling in the gaps.

Count on your fingers to check your answers.

6 + 4 =

10 + ☐ = 16   21 + 9 =

16 + 3 =   52 + ☐ = 54

5 + ☐ = 5   48 + 2 =

When you are adding, it doesn't matter which way round the sum goes. The answer to 53 + 5 is the same as 5 + 53. So you can 'count on' 5 starting at 53. Write in the answer...

5 + 53 =

Now try these sums...

1 + 101 =   8 + 35 =

NOW TEST YOURSELF WITH SOME FUN PUZZLES.

MERLIN MOUSE'S BRAIN TEASERS

Merlin is playing with three of his brothers. Five more come along to play. How many is he playing with now?

Yum-yum!

Merlin has found **5** lumps of cheese in the kitchen. Then he finds **2** more. How many lumps of cheese does he have?

One of these is NOT a term that means 'add'. Circle it.

PLUS   +   PRODUCT   TOTAL   INCREASE

Merlin is **2** years old.
How old will he be in **4** years' time?

Merlin and his sister Mudge are playing a game. They get **2** points every time they roll a ball into a bucket and **5** points every time they roll it through the mouse hole.

Here are their scores...

	Merlin	Mudge
Bucket	2	1
Hole	1	2

Points

Who has won the game?.................................

NOW YOU KNOW HOW TO COUNT ON!

SUBTRACTION IN ACTION

Here are Whiz-Bang's wands again to show you how to subtract by counting back. Number lines are useful when subtracting single numbers (units).

To do the sum **4 - 3**, start at **4** and COUNT BACK **3**.

3   2   1   -

1   2   3   4   5   6   7   8   9   10

So, **4 - 3 = 1**

Just like counting on, it doesn't matter where the number line begins. Try this sum below, using this number line.

25   26   27   28   29   30   31   32   33

Counting back is the INVERSE (opposite) of counting on.

33 - 5 =

MAGIC MEANINGS

When you see a sum like this: **5 - 3**

It means:

Five **SUBTRACT** three

Five **TAKE AWAY** three

Five **MINUS** three

Five **DECREASED** by three

Five **LESS** three

The **DIFFERENCE** between five and three

And the answer is **2**!

When you see the ➖ sign you know you have to take away.

READY TO SUBTRACT?

TAKE AWAY ONE

Kit Cat is eating crunchies. She has 8 in her bowl and she eats one at a time. Count back with her.

8 - 1 =

7 - 1 =

6 - 1 =

5 - 1 =

4 - 1 =

3 - 1 =

2 - 1 =

Kit is now sad. After she eats the next one, how many will she have left?

MORE THAN TEN

Kit can take away from double and triple digits!

11 - 1 =

20 - 1 =

[ ] - 1 = 23

13 - 1 =

[ ] - 1 = 20

32 - 1 =

[ ] - 1 = 0

100 - 1 =

101 - 1 =

I count back in my head.

READY FOR SOME MORE?

17

COUNTING BACK

Kit Cat likes doing easy sums by counting back. For you, it is even easier as you can use your fingers to help you.

4 - 1 =

6 - 2 =

10 - 5 =

8 - 4 =

9 - 6 =

Here are three bowls of cat crunchies. If Kit eats three crunchies from each bowl, how many will be left? Cross out three to find out (the first one has been done for you).

7 - 3 = 4

10 - 3 =

4 - 3 =

Now try these sums.

9 - 2 = ▢

10 - ▢ = 2

26 - 5 = ▢

8 - ▢ = 1

32 - 3 = ▢

68 - ▢ = 59

22 - 2 = ▢

13 - ▢ = 8

80 - 7 = ▢

Use your fingers as a number line.

Unlike adding, it DOES matter which way round the sum goes when you are subtracting. The answer to **2 - 1** is not same as **1 - 2**. If you have two sweets and you eat one, you have one left. But if you have one sweet you cannot eat two!

NOW TEST YOURSELF WITH SOME FUN PUZZLES

KIT CAT'S BRAIN TEASERS

Kit and her friend Claudius are watching birds in the garden. There are **5** birds, but **3** fly away.
How many are left? **2**

Kit has **5** toys. Claudius has one less than Kit. How many toys does Claudius have? **4**

Take away **5** from **6**. **1**

Circle the term that does NOT mean subtract.

MINUS - INCREASE TAKE AWAY DECREASE

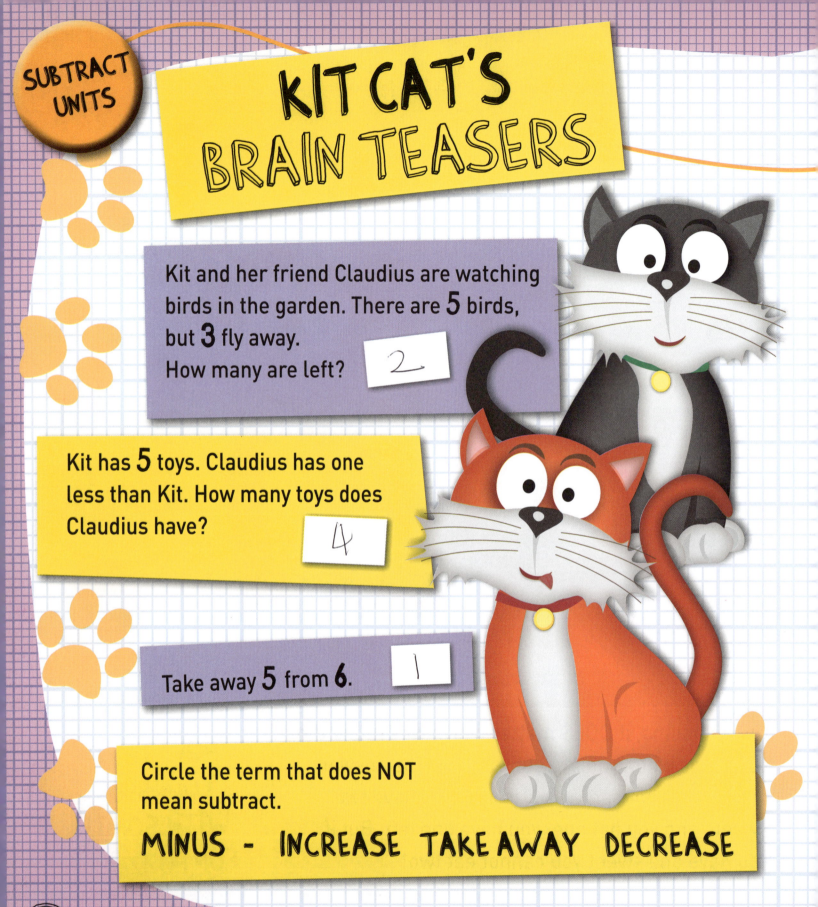

Kit has made **20** muddy paw prints on the kitchen floor.
Her owner has mopped up **8** already.
How many are left?

12

Like all cats, Kit and Claudius were both born with **9** lives.
Kit has lost **2**, and Claudius has lost **4**.
How many do they each have left?

Kit 6   Claudius 5

If **6** is **8** decreased by **2**,
what is **9** decreased by **3**?

You are a
clever cat!

Subtract **1** from **6**   5

NOW YOU KNOW HOW TO COUNT BACK!

21

REMEMBER IT!

Ready for a recap on how to add and subtract units by counting on and back?

Try doing them in your head, but if you need to, use a number line or your fingers to help you.

$11 + 3 = \boxed{}$

$90 - 2 = \boxed{}$

$\boxed{} + 5 = 10$

$18 + \boxed{} = 26$

$3 - \boxed{} = 0$

Whiz-Bang has **4** wands in his hand. If he decreases that number by **3**, how many wands will he be holding? $\boxed{}$

Whiz-Bang is making potions. He has made **10** but needs to increase that number by **5**. How many potions will he have? $\boxed{}$

Merlin had **10** berries. He eats **3** and then he eats another **2**. Cross them out to find out how many he has left?

10 - 3 - 2 = [ ]

Merlin is playing hide-and-seek with his **8** brothers and **8** sisters. He has found **3** of them. How many more does he need to find? [ ]

Kit is making more muddy paw prints. She has taken **14** steps. How many paw prints will there be if she takes another...

3 steps? [ ]

7 steps? [ ]

WELL DONE! YOU ARE GREAT!

NUMBER BONDS TO 10

Knowing number bonds is more handy than...

A hook?

Pirate Blacktooth knows all the numbers that add up to 10. Here they are. These are known as 'number bonds' so learn them well!

$$9 + 1 = 10$$
$$8 + 2 = 10$$
$$7 + 3 = 10$$
$$6 + 4 = 10$$
$$5 + 5 = 10$$
$$4 + 6 = 10$$
$$3 + 7 = 10$$
$$2 + 8 = 10$$
$$1 + 9 = 10$$

24

LEARNING NUMBER BONDS

When you know your number bonds, it makes adding easier. Join up the coins that add up to **10**, then check your answers, using the grid opposite.

4   7   6   3   9

2   8   5   1   5

Now fill in these gaps...

$9 + \boxed{} = 10$

$\boxed{} + 7 = 10$

$5 + \boxed{} = 10$

$\boxed{} + 4 = 10$

$8 + \boxed{} = 10$

ALWAYS PLAY SPOT THE BOND!

25

ADDING NUMBER BONDS

Pirate Blacktooth has five bags of coins.
Each bag must contain ten coins. If they don't, draw them in.

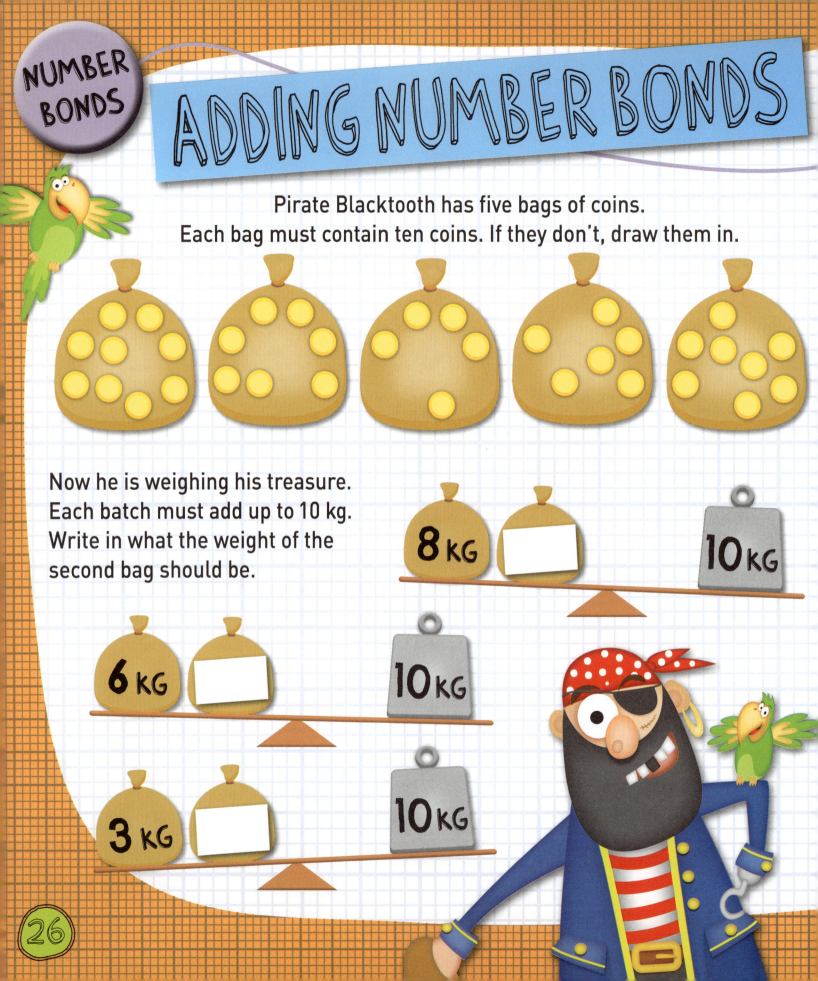

Now he is weighing his treasure.
Each batch must add up to 10 kg.
Write in what the weight of the
second bag should be.

8 KG ☐ **10** KG

6 KG ☐ **10** KG

3 KG ☐ **10** KG

PIRATE BLACKTOOTH'S
SHIVERING SUMS

Try doing these sums as quickly as possible.

$7 + \boxed{} = 10$

$\boxed{} + 5 = 10$

$2 + \boxed{} = 10$

$9 + \boxed{} = 10$

$\boxed{} + 3 = 10$

$5 + \boxed{} = 10$

$1 + \boxed{} = 10$

$\boxed{} + 4 = 10$

$6 + \boxed{} = 10$

$8 + \boxed{} = 10$

Arr! You've passed your first pirate lesson.

READY FOR MORE PIRATE PRACTICE?

SUBTRACTING NUMBER BONDS

Pirate Blacktooth has to buy provisions for his journey. Here are his bags of 10 coins. If he buys each item, how many coins will he have in each bag?

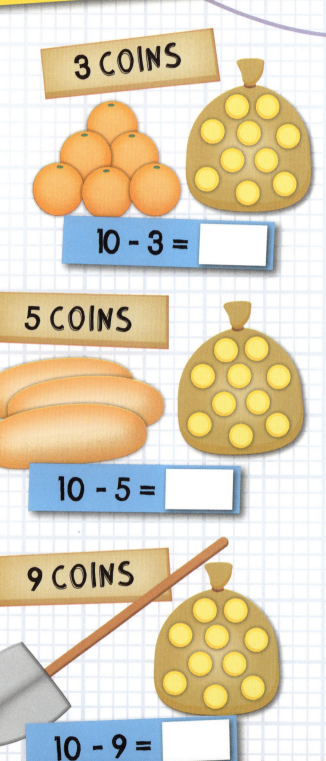

3 COINS

$10 - 3 =$ _____

8 COINS

$10 - 8 =$ _____

5 COINS

$10 - 5 =$ _____

4 COINS

$10 - 4 =$ _____

9 COINS

$10 - 9 =$ _____

PIRATE BLACKTOOTH'S SUBTRACTION SUMS

Try doing these as quickly as possible.

10 - 2 = ☐

10 - ☐ = 5

10 - 3 = ☐

10 - 8 = ☐

10 - ☐ = 3

10 - 9 = ☐

10 - ☐ = 2

10 - 4 = ☐

10 - 5 = ☐

10 - ☐ = 9

Shiver me timbers! You've passed your second pirate lesson.

NOW FOR SOME PIRATE PUZZLES.

PIRATE BLACKTOOTH'S BRAIN TEASERS

Pirate Blacktooth has found lots of gold coins. He adds them up using number bonds. Do the same, crossing out the coins as you go, keeping count of the number of bonds on your fingers or in your head.

1	8	2	5	5
6	7	9	1	4
7	9	3	2	6
3	7	5	4	8
9	1	2	3	8

How many tens does he have? ☐

One coin is left over. What is its value? ☐

If Blacktooth has **6** cannon balls, how many does he buy to make **10**? ☐

If he then fires **3** at Pirate Bonny's ship, how many does he have left? ☐

Can you balance these pirate scales?

5 KG [ ] 10 KG

9 KG [ ] 10 KG

Blacktooth is doing what he likes best – piling up his jewels. How many must he add to each pile to make three piles of ten?

6 + [ ]   9 + [ ]   7 + [ ]

Try these sums:

[ ] - 3 KG = 7 KG

10 KG - 2 KG = [ ]

10 KG - 1 KG = [ ]

Aye, aye! You've passed pirate lesson number three!

YOU'RE GETTING GOOD AT NUMBER BONDS.

DOUBLE TROUBLE

Learning doubles is another way of making addition easier. Here they are...

1 + 1 = **2**

2 + 2 = **4**

3 + 3 = **6**

4 + 4 = **8**

5 + 5 = **10**

6 + 6 = **12**

7 + 7 = **14**

8 + 8 = **16**

9 + 9 = **18**

10 + 10 = **20**

Now cover up the answers. Can you remember them?

Parrot Pete is a doubling expert. If he's good, Blacktooth doubles the number of peanuts he gives him. Here's what Blacktooth gives Pete on Monday...

$5 + 5 =$ 10

On Tuesday, Blacktooth gives Pete one extra for being REALLY good. As this is a near double, Pete can simply add one more.

$5 + 6 =$

On Wednesday, Blacktooth doesn't have quite enough peanuts to double the number. He's one short, so how many does Pete get?

$5 + 4 =$

READY TO DO THE OPPOSITE?

HALF MEASURES

Halving is the INVERSE of doubling, which means it is the opposite action. Can you halve these numbers, by splitting them into equal numbers?

4 = (2) + (2)

20 = ( ) + ( )

12 = ( ) + ( )

10 = ( ) + ( )

6 = ( ) + ( )

16 = ( ) + ( )

8 = ( ) + ( )

14 = ( ) + ( )

2 = ( ) + ( )

18 = ( ) + ( )

Check your answers by adding them together.

34

LEARNING WITH PARROT PETE

I love counting seeds!

When Pete is naughty, Blacktooth halves the number of seeds he gives Pete. On Thursday, Blacktooth was going to give Pete six seeds but he only gives him half.

6 - 3 = 3

On Friday, Pete is REALLY naughty, so Blacktooth takes away one more. As this is a near double, Pete can work this out by simply taking one away from half.

6 - 4 =

READY FOR SOME PRACTICE?

35

PARROT PETE'S PARROT PRACTICE

Pete needs help with these sums.
They are either doubles or near doubles.

Who's a clever kid then?

$8 + 8 = \boxed{}$

$8 + 7 = \boxed{}$

$10 + 10 = \boxed{}$

$10 + \boxed{} = 21$

$\boxed{} + 3 = 6$

$3 + 4 = \boxed{}$

$\boxed{} + 5 = 10$

$6 + \boxed{} = 11$

$7 + 7 = \boxed{}$

$6 + 7 = \boxed{}$

12 = 6 + ☐
13 = 6 + ☐

Now help him with these ones. They are either halves or near halves. Can you fill in the missing numbers?

2 = 1 + ☐
3 = 1 + ☐

4 = 2 + ☐
5 = 2 + ☐

10 = 5 + ☐
9 = 5 + ☐

8 = 4 + ☐
7 = 4 + ☐

If you got the last one right, can you do this one?

80 = 40 + ☐
70 = 40 + ☐

NOW TEST YOURSELF WITH SOME FUN PUZZLES.

PARROT PETE'S BRAIN TEASERS

If you get stuck, go back to page 32!

Parrot Pete is **6** years old. The ship's cat is double his age. How old is she?

Pete cost Blacktooth **16** gold coins. The other parrots cost half that amount. How much did they cost?

It takes **8** seconds for Pete to fly to the crow's nest. How long does it take him to fly there and back?

seconds

If double **9** is **18**, what is **9 + 10**?

If half a pizza has **3** slices, how many does a whole pizza have?

Parrot Pete has done a poop in Pirate Blacktooth's dinner! Blacktooth was going to give him **10** peanuts and **20** seeds, but Blacktooth halves that amount. How many of each does Pete get?

Peanuts ⬭   Seeds ⬭

YOU'RE A SHIP-SHAPE PIRATE'S MATE.

REMEMBER IT!

Can you remember your number bonds?
Here are some sums to refresh your memory.

$$10 - \boxed{} = 8$$

$$4 + \boxed{} = 10$$

$$3 + \boxed{} = 10$$

$$10 - 1 = \boxed{}$$

$$10 - 5 = \boxed{}$$

Which two numbers do not add up to 10?

5 and 5   1 and 8   3 and 7

9 and 1   6 and 4

Here are Pirate Blacktooth's scales. Write in the weight that will balance them?

2 KG   [ ]   10 KG

That's great, ship-mate!

Now let's test your halving and doubling...

Blacktooth has **20** diamonds, **18** rubies, **8** sapphires and **14** emeralds in his treasure chest. His arch rival Pirate Bonny, steals half of each. How many does he have left?

Diamonds ◯

Sapphires ◯

Rubies ◯

Emeralds ◯

It takes Parrot Pete **3** hours to fly from one island to the next. How many hours does it take him to fly there and back? ◯

If **10 + 10 = 20**, what is **11 + 10**? ◯

ARR... YOU'RE AN ADDING STAR.

TENS AND UNITS

Bella Butterfly is an expert at tens and units. She has to be – she has **6** dots on the left wing and **6** on the right. Add them together and they make **12**!

$$6 \quad + \quad 6 \quad = 12$$

To make counting easy, we group every set of **10** together and the units are what's left over.

$$6 \quad + \quad 6 \quad = 10 + 2$$

So there is one set of 10 with 2 units left over. This is shown below, with a tens column and a units column.

TENS	UNITS
1	2

This makes 12.

TIME FOR PRACTICE

Bella has made a test for you. For the groups below, write how many tens and units there are.

TENS UNITS

TENS UNITS

TENS UNITS

Now try these...

In each of the numbers, circle the tens.

24 95 73 55 68 17

Now circle the units.

65 84 24 66 57 48

Brilliant!

READY FOR SOME MORE PRACTICE?

43

TIME TO ADD TENS

When adding 10 to any number, you don't need to count on every time. You just need to add another group of 10 to the tens column. Try these sums.

23 + 10 = ◯

42 + 10 = ◯

10 + 57 = ◯

10 + 51 = ◯

64 + 10 = ◯

43 + 10 = ◯

Remember, when adding 10, the units stay the same.

TIME TO SUBTRACT TENS

When subtracting 10 from any number, you don't need to count back. You just take away a group of 10 from the tens column. Try these sums.

Good luck!

67 - 10 = ◯

18 - 10 = ◯

21 - 10 = ◯

33 - 10 = ◯

49 - 10 = ◯

82 - 10 = ◯

When subtracting 10, the units also stay the same.

READY FOR SOME PUZZLES?

45

BELLA BUTTERFLY'S BRAIN TEASERS

Good luck!

Bella Butterfly has collected **35** petals. She collects **10** more. How many does she have?

45

What is the sum of **20** and **10**?

30

Which of these numbers is the same as five tens and six units?

56   **65**   **5106**   **506**

56

Bella's friend Colin Caterpillar comes to stay for a week, then he stays ten days more. How many days does he stay in total?

At the bug ball, there are **23** butterflies, **10** grasshoppers and **10** caterpillars.

How many bugs are there in total?

43

If the grasshoppers leave, how many bugs are left?

33

If the caterpillars leave as well, how many bugs are left?

23

If all the caterpillars and grasshoppers go to buy a lollipop each, how many lollipops do they buy?

20

GREAT ADDING AND TAKING AWAY!

47

TENS AND HUNDREDS

Try these ones!

Hattie Hen is the egg-laying queen of her farm. She lays **10** eggs a week. Here's the farmer's record. Can you fill in the missing totals?

Week	Eggs	Total
1	10	10
2	10	20
3	10	
4	10	40
5	10	
6	10	60
7	10	
8	10	80
9	10	
10	10	100

When a group of ten is added to 90, you get 10 tens, which is 100 (a triple digit number).

WHAT ARE HUNDREDS?

The number **100** can be written with a hundreds column, a tens column and a units column. It is one group of a hundred, with no tens and no units.

HUNDREDS	TENS	UNITS
1	0	0

See what happens if you add **10** to **100**.

HUNDREDS	TENS	UNITS
1	1	0

So... **100 + 10 = 110**

Look what happens if you add **90** to **110**. Write in the answer below.

HUNDREDS	TENS	UNITS
2	0	0

So... **110 + 90 =**

Remember 10 tens make a hundred.

NOW FOR SOME PRACTICE.

49

TIME TO ADD 10s AND 100s

Help Hattie Hen with these sums.

H	T	U
110 + 50 = ⬭⬭⬭

H	T	U
200 + 200 = ⬭⬭⬭

H	T	U
110 + 10 = ⬭⬭⬭

H	T	U
160 + 30 = ⬭⬭⬭

Cock-a-doodle-doo! Here's more to do.

210 + 70 = ⬭

120 + 60 = ⬭

300 + 40 = ⬭

Try this one, if you're feeling clucky...

190 + 20 = ⬭

TIME TO SUBTRACT 10s AND 100s

Hattie is now trying to subtract 100s and 10s.
Can you help with these sums?

120 - 20 =   H T U ◯◯◯

650 - 200 =   H T U ◯◯◯

270 - 50 =   H T U ◯◯◯

150 - 40 =   H T U ◯◯◯

Cluck-cluck! Check the answer if you're stuck.

340 - 30 = ◯   20 - 20 = ◯

Finding them hard? Don't flap. Just look in the back!

Try this one, if you're feeling plucky...

330 - 110 = ◯

CRACKING EFFORT. WELL DONE!

51

HATTIE HEN'S BRAIN TEASERS

After four weeks, Hattie has laid **40** eggs. The farmer gives **20** to his mum and **10** to his brother. How many does he have left?

The farmer has egg boxes that can contain **10** eggs each.

He packs **5** boxes. How many eggs are inside?

If he gives away **2** boxes, how many eggs does he have left?

What is the sum of three tens and three tens?

Which of these numbers is the same as three hundreds and five tens?

315   35   3005   350   530

What is **80** plus **100** plus **10**?

Circle the sum that has a different answer to the rest.

80 - 30   70 - 30   40 + 10

100 - 50   30 + 20   90 - 40

Cluck-cluck! Check the answer if you're stuck.

EGG-CELLENT JOB!

53

NUMBER BONDS

NUMBER BONDS TO 20

All good pirates know the numbers that make up 10, but really clever pirates know them up to 20! Here they are. Look at them, learn them, cover them up and remember them.

$$11 + 9 = 20$$
$$12 + 8 = 20$$
$$13 + 7 = 20$$
$$14 + 6 = 20$$
$$15 + 5 = 20$$
$$16 + 4 = 20$$
$$17 + 3 = 20$$
$$18 + 2 = 20$$
$$19 + 1 = 20$$

Can you see the difference between number bonds to 10 and to 20? See page 24.

LEARNING NUMBER BONDS

If you look at the units, you'll see that they are the same as the number bonds that make 10. That's because $11 + 9$ is the same as $10 + 1 + 9$, which is two tens. Here's the sum again written in columns.

Spotting number bonds makes sums easier.

TENS	UNITS
1	1
	9 +
2	0

Can you circle the sum that does not add up to 20?

19 + 1

13 + 7

2 + 18

5 + 15

6 + 13

I SPY A CLEVER PIRATE.

55

NUMBER BONDS

FIND THE NUMBER BONDS TO 20

Pirate Bonny is Blacktooth's arch enemy. She is hoping to outwit him with her quick maths skills. Can you help?

$17 + \boxed{} = 20$

$\boxed{} + 4 = 20$

$1 + \boxed{} = 20$

$\boxed{} + 15 = 20$

$18 + \boxed{} = 20$

Now try this sum...

$22 + 8 = \boxed{}$

A pirate salute to you, if you got the last one right.

PIRATE BONNY'S BRAINY SUMS

Okay me hearties, have a go at this little lot.

$$20 - \boxed{} = 14$$

$$20 - \boxed{} = 13$$

$$20 - \boxed{} = 11$$

$$20 - \boxed{} = 12$$

$$20 - \boxed{} = 10$$

Circle the two numbers whose sum does not add up to **20**.

11 AND 8

6 AND 14

15 AND 5

18 AND 2

13 AND 7

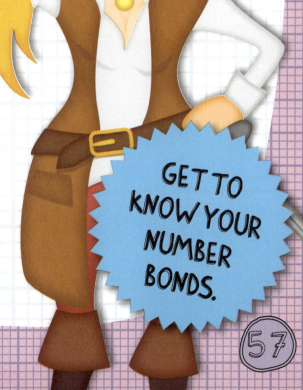

GET TO KNOW YOUR NUMBER BONDS.

DIFFERENCES

WHAT'S THE DIFFERENCE?

If you are asked the difference between one great white shark and three little fish, what would you say? Size? Teeth? One eats the other? Well, in maths the right answer is ... 2!

1 SHARK

3 FISH

The difference between 6 fish and 2 fish is a hungry tummy!

In maths, the question really is, what is the **difference in number**? If there are 3 fish and 1 shark, the difference in number is 2.

The difference between **6** fish and **2** fish is **4** fish. You can see it on this number line.

58

FINDING THE DIFFERENCE

There are many ways to find the difference between two numbers. To find the difference between **20** and **17** you could count on...

15 16 17 18 19 20 21 22

You could also count back...

15 16 17 18 19 20 21 22

You could write the sum down...

20 - 17 =

Or you could do the sum in your head. (Remember your number bonds?)

Which ever way you choose, the answer is the same. Write it here...

COOL CALCULATING!

DIFFERENCES

SOLVING SUMS WITH SID

Sid Shark has spied two groups of fish.
What is the difference between the two?

The difference is [ ]

What is the difference between the green fish and [ ] **blue fish below?**

How many more fish need to join the blue fish to make the difference 4? [ ]

You can draw them in to check your answer.

MORE SUMS

How many of these pairs of bubbles have a difference of 5. ☐

1 6　9 4　19 13　11 6　7 2　12 5

By working out the differences between the numbers, can you finish these sequences?

| 1 | 3 | 5 | 7 | 9 | ☐ |

| 16 | 13 | 10 | 7 | 4 | ☐ |

| 6 | 7 | 9 | 12 | 16 | ☐ |

Now find the differences between these numbers.

14 AND 17 ☐

18 AND 6 ☐

2 AND 9 ☐

NOW IT'S TEST TIME...

61

DIFFERENCES

SID SHARK'S
BRAIN TEASERS

Sid is **2** metres long. His dad is **4** metres long. What's the difference between the two?

METRES

When Sid was a year old, he had **32** teeth. Now he has **40** teeth. Find the difference.

Sid is sharing out his shell collection between his three brothers.

A   B C

How many does he need to add to **B** and **C** to make all three piles the same?

B C

The sharks are playing underwater football with the dolphins, but the dolphins have a bigger team. If there are **11** sharks and the difference between the teams is **8**, how many dolphins are there?

Five of the dolphins get sent off! What's the difference now?

Sid swims the first half of a **400**-metre race in **20** seconds. If he takes **45** seconds to finish the race, how much slower does he swim the second half?

SECONDS

Finish this sequence...

20   21   23   26   30

GREAT WORK.

63

REMEMBER IT!

Time to see if you can remember all about 10s and 100s, number bonds and differences.

If Whiz-Bang has **10** green bottles and **5** purple bottles, what is the difference?

Pirate Bonny is weighing her gold. On one side she has **50** kg and on the other she has **20** kg. Circle the weight that will balance the scales?

20 KG   50 KG

10 KG

20 KG

30 KG

Last week, Hattie Hen laid **7** eggs. This week she laid **10**. What's the difference?

Sid Shark joins a swimathon with his friends.

Sid does **40** laps to the island and back.

Chuckles does **30** laps

Little Blue does **20** laps.

How many laps do they do in total?

Find the number bonds!

Circle the two numbers whose sum would not end in 0 (zero).

41   8

22   8

6   34

55   5

63   7

TOP OF THE CLASS!

DOUBLE DIGITS

ADDING DOUBLE DIGITS

When adding double digits that have both tens and units, the easiest way is to add the tens first and then the units.

$17 + 12 = 10 + 10 = 20$ (2 tens)

$7 + 2 = 9$ (9 units)

Then add the two answers together.

$17 + 12 = 20 + 9 = 29$

Can you do this one?

$11 + 13 = 10 + 10 =$ ☐

$1 + 3 =$ ☐

Add the answers together.

$11 + 13 =$ ☐ $+$ ☐ $=$ ☐

When you add double digits, sometimes the units add up to 10 or more than 10. See what happens.

$17 + 13 = 10 + 10 = 20$ (2 tens)

$7 + 3 = 10$ (1 ten)

So there are 3 tens and 0 units. $17 + 13 = 20 + 10 = 30$

66

There is another way to add tricky double digit sums. It's called 'rounding' and it's useful when one or both of the numbers are near tens, such as $19 + 19$.

You already know that $20 + 20 = 40$.

You know that 19 is one less than 20.

So if you round up the sum to one you can do easily, you simply take away the units you added from the answer.

Here's how it works...

$19 + 1 + 19 + 1$ is the same as $20 + 20$.

So, $19 + 19 = 40 - 1 - 1 = 38$

Can you do this one?

$29 + 19 = \boxed{}$

READY FOR SOME PRACTICE?

ZEE THE ZEBRA'S PRACTICE SUMS

Try doing the sums in your head.

Zee the Zebra has come up with these sums for you. First add the tens, then the units and add the answers together.

24 + 15 = 39

82 + 16 = 988

18 + 11 = 29

23 + 23 = 466

31 + 24 = 55

55 + 14 = 69

57 + 22 = 79

21 + 42 = 63

66 + 33 = 99

Now try this one...

79 + 11 = 80

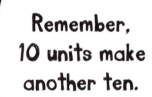

Remember, 10 units make another ten.

ZEE'S ROUNDING SUMS

29 + 29 = 68

39 + 19 = 59

49 + 39 =

109 + 29 =

59 + 19 =

19 + 69 =

79 + 19 =

49 + 49 =

29 + 49 =

If you round up by 1 you take away 1 from the answer. If you round up by 2 you take away 2!

Now try this one...

19 + 18 =

ZIPPETY ZEBRAS, YOU'RE GETTING GOOD!

69

SUBTRACTING DOUBLE DIGITS

You still ADD the answers.

You can use the same method of subtracting the tens and units when subtracting double digits, but ONLY if both digits of the first number are BIGGER than those in the second number.

$36 - 12 = 30 - 10 = 20$ (2 tens)

$6 - 2 = 4$ (4 units)

Then add the two answers together.

$36 - 12 = 20 + 4 = 24$

Can you do this one?

$26 - 15 = 20 - 10 = \boxed{}$

$6 - 5 = \boxed{}$

Add the answers together.

$26 - 15 = \boxed{} + \boxed{} = \boxed{}$

ROUNDING UP AND DOWN

You can also use rounding with subtraction. Here's a tricky sum.

$$90 - 19 =$$

With subtracting, when you round UP, you ADD to the answer. When you round down, you TAKE AWAY.

You already know that $90 - 20 = 70$.

As **19** is one less than **20**, you are taking away one less from **90**, so your answer will be one more.

$$90 - 19 = 70 + 1 = 71$$

With subtraction, rounding down can also be helpful. Here's another tricky sum.

$$90 - 21 =$$

As **21** is one more than **20**, you are taking away one more from **90**, so your answer will be one less.

$$90 - 21 = 70 - 1 =$$

READY FOR SOME PRACTICE?

GEORGIE GIRAFFE TAKES AWAY

On the other side of the plain, Georgie Giraffe is struggling with her own sums. Can you help her by subtracting the tens and then the units?

36 - 25 =

28 - 11 =

67 - 31 =

32 - 12 =

54 - 22 =

97 - 86 =

79 - 52 =

21 - 10 =

44 - 13 =

85 - 23 =

Try doing the sums in your head.

Don't forget, 100 is the same as 10 tens.

Now try this one...

101 - 91 =

GEORGIE'S ROUNDING SUMS

ROUNDING UP SUMS

As you are rounding up, you ADD 1 to the answer.

70 - 19 =

60 - 29 =

30 - 19 =

100 - 89 =

ROUNDING DOWN SUMS

As you are rounding down, you TAKE AWAY 1 from the answer.

80 - 21 =

50 - 31 =

40 - 11 =

100 - 11 =

JUMPING GIRAFFES. YOU ARE GETTING IT.

GEORGIE'S NUMBER LINES

Georgie Giraffe also uses number lines and differences to do REALLY tricky sums like

$$73 - 54 =$$

Here's how she does it...

Counting on from **54** to **60** is easy. The answer is **6**.

The difference between **60** and **70** is **10**.

From **70** to **73**, you count on **3**.

So breaking down the sum on a number line into easy chunks makes a difficult sum much easier. The difference between

73 and **54** is... $6 + 10 + 3 = 19$

GEORGIE'S JUMPING SUMS

Work out the answer to these sums, using the number lines.

92 – 75 =

5 + 10 + 2

75   80   90   92

81 – 38 =

See if you can do the next sums, putting your own numbers on the number line.

+   +

38   40   80   81

74 – 57 =

+   +

57   74

TRICKY JUST GOT EASY! GOOD JOB.

ZEE AND GEORGIE'S BRAIN TEASERS

Zee and Georgie are at the watering hole. Zee has taken **34** sips and Georgie has taken **35**. How many have they taken in total?

Georgie is a super-fast runner.
She can run **30** kph.
Zee can run **19** kph.

What is the difference?

Georgie eats **100** leaves a day in the winter and **65** leaves a day in the summer. How many fewer does she eat in the summer?

There are **75** zebras in Zee's herd: **54** are female. How many are male?

Of the **75** zebras, **10** are babies and a further **15** are young ones. How many is that in total?

So, if the rest are adults, how many are there?

It's the night of the Great Plains Quiz. Each correct answer scores 2 points.

The zebras have **34** points.

The giraffes have **22** points.

The smarty-pants elephants have **58** points.

By how many points are the elephants beating:

The zebras?   The giraffes?

Are the elephants beating both teams put together?   YES   NO

THAT'S WILD!

BIG SUMS

ADDING BIG AND LONG SUMS

This is Professor Chipmunk. He has built a magnificent maths machine. He can put in any number or any number of numbers, and it will add them up for him.

He puts in these super-sized sums.

$$45 + 320 + 210 =$$ $$902 + 72 + 13 =$$

| | 45 | 210 |
| | 320 | |

H	T	U
3 2	2 1 4	0 0 5

● **ADD**

HUNDREDS	5		
TENS		7	
UNITS			5

| **TOTAL** | 5 | 7 | 5 |

| | 72 | 13 |
| | 902 | |

H	T	U
9	0 7 1	2 2 3

● **ADD**

HUNDREDS	9		
TENS		8	
UNITS			7

| **TOTAL** | 9 | 8 | 7 |

78

THE MAGNIFICENT MATHS MACHINE

Can you fill in the answer windows, based on the numbers going into the machine at the top?

22   4
720

H T U
7   2   0
    2   2
        4

● ADD

HUNDREDS
TENS
UNITS

TOTAL

73   23
203

H   T   U
    7   3
2   2   3
    0   3

● ADD

HUNDREDS
TENS
UNITS

TOTAL

OUTSTANDING!

YOU'RE GETTING IT!

THE PROFESSOR'S PRACTICE

Can you work out these super-sized sums using the magnificent maths machine?

$$12 + 560 + 215 =$$
$$702 + 31 + 124 =$$

12   560
215

H   T   U

● ADD

HUNDREDS
TENS
UNITS

TOTAL

702   31
124

H   T   U

● ADD

HUNDREDS
TENS
UNITS

TOTAL

Now try this one without the machine...

$$653 +$$
$$33 +$$
$$12 =$$

Write your answer here. → _____

BRILLIANT BIG SUMS

Try this sum...

$$201 + 53 + 102 =$$

ADD

HUNDREDS

TENS

UNITS

TOTAL

Now try these four sums without the machine...

Write your answers here. →

$$317 +$$
$$60 +$$
$$2 =$$
_____
_____

$$466 +$$
$$12 +$$
$$1 =$$
_____
_____

$$555 +$$
$$31 +$$
$$100 =$$
_____
_____

$$805 +$$
$$23 +$$
$$20 =$$
_____
_____

MAGNIFICENT!

REMEMBER IT!

Are adding and subtracting double and triple digits easy-peasy now? Let's see how you get on with this little recap.

$65 + 12 =$

$72 - 61 =$

$70 + 22 =$

$55 + 25 =$

$87 - 64 =$

$33 + 33 =$

$69 + 69 =$ 128

$59 + 49 =$

$109 + 29 =$

Use rounding for the sums above and below.

$30 - 21 =$

$90 - 39 =$

$100 - 51 =$

If Georgie collects **62** ostrich feathers and Zee collects **37**, how many do they have in total?

Using the number line below, can you do this tricky sum?

62 - 47 = ☐

47   50   60   62

Use Professor Chipmunk's magnificent maths machine to do this sum...

212 + 121 + 221 =

Now try this one without the machine...

207 +
602 +
80 =
———————
———————

212   121
221

H   T   U

☐ ☐ ☐

🟢 ADD

HUNDREDS ☐
TENS ☐
UNITS ☐

TOTAL ☐ ☐ ☐

MONEY MATTERS

This is Cool Dog. He sells ice cream at the local park to the other dogs. He has to be quick at adding up and giving change. Here are his prices...

COOL CONE	CHOC CONE	T-BONE	CHOC TUB
15P	20P	25P	25P

His first customers ask for two Choc Cones. In his head, Cool Dog adds it up...

20p + 20p = 40p

They give him £1.

Knowing that £1 is the same as 100P, Cool Dog works out how much change to give them. 100p - 40p = 60p

His next customers ask for a Cool Cone and a T-Bone.
Cool Dog works out what to charge them.

They give him **50p**. What change should he give them?

50p - 40p = | 10 |

15p + 25p = 40p

More customers want two Cool Cones and a Choc Tub. What should Cool Dog charge them for the three ice creams?

15p + 15p + 25p = | 55 |

They give him **60p**. What change should he give them? | |

READY FOR SOME PRACTICE?

85

COOL DOG'S MONEY PRACTICE

You can use a piece of paper to work out the sums.

Here is Cool Dog's price list again.

COOL CONE	CHOC CONE	T-BONE	CHOC TUB
15p	20p	25p	25p

Below is a shopping list with the money the customer has to pay with. Cool Dog adds up the total and calculates the change. Can you do the same for the two lists on the next page?

50p

	COST
2 COOL CONES	30p
1 CHOC CONE	20p
TOTAL	50p
CHANGE	0

86

COOL DOG'S CALCULATIONS

MONEY

£1 50p   COST

2 COOL CONES
2 CHOC CONES
1 CHOC TUB
1 T-BONE

TOTAL
CHANGE   £ 1 50p

£1   COST

1 T-BONE
1 CHOC TUB

TOTAL
CHANGE   2 Ph

If you have **£1**, what is the maximum number of ice creams you can buy?   2

Which ice cream would you buy?

WELL DONE!

87

COOL DOG'S BRAIN TEASERS

If one Cool Cone is **15p** and one Choc Tub is **25p**.
How much is that in total?

40

At the end of the afternoon, Cool Dog has taken **£5.10**.
Yesterday he took **£6.20**.
What's the difference?

difference

A customer comes with **50p** and needs **3** ice creams.
She has two options. How much change does she get with each?

OPTION 1

CHANGE

5

15p 15p 15p

OPTION 2

CHANGE

0

15p 15p 20p

You have these coins in your pocket. How much do they add up to?

You buy two Choc Tubs at **25p** each. How much do you have left?

50

Don't forget that £1.00 is the same as 100p.

Cool Dog has taken **£5.10**.
He needs to buy some things for the following day. Here's what he buys and how much they cost:

BOWLS	£1.00
FUEL	£2.50
SPRINKLES	25p
SAUCE	25p
TOTAL	4.00

How much does he have left? *000*

THAT'S COOL!

THE ULTIMATE TEST

Are you ready to test yourself using all the techniques you've learned in this book? If you write your answers on a piece of paper, you can test yourself again. Ready?

Remember... count on, count back and number bonds.

$3 + 6 = 9$

$9 + 2 = 11$

$10 + 7 = 17$

$5 + 5 = 10$

Circle the term that has nothing to do with subtraction.

TAKE AWAY   MINUS   DECREASE   TIMES   DIFFERENCE

Can you halve **20**? 10

Can you double **8**? 16

$60 - 20 = 40$

$20 + 10 = 30$

$10 + 35 = 45$

What's the difference between **10** and **15**? it5

Balance these scales

 8 KG 2 KG   10 KG

78 + 11 = 84   100 - 80 = 20   68 + 2 =

65 - 35 = 30   92 - 71 = 21   44 - 13 =

75 — 60P

If you have **75p** and the ice creams are **20p** each, how many can you buy?

How much change would you get?

Remember ten units makes a ten.

How many pairs of bubbles have a difference of **8**.

22   20   58   5

14   12   50   13

Thinking about the magical maths machine, can you do this sum?

100 10 U

240 +
34 +
202 =
_____
476

Use the number line to do this tricky sum.

103 - 77 =

77   103

Now check your answers. Are you a marvellous maths magician or still a sorcerer's apprentice?

WHIZ-BANG'S ANSWERS

Page 5
43 - 9 = 34

Page 6
37 + 3 = 40

Page 8
2 + 1 = 3
3 + 1 = 4
4 + 1 = 5
5 + 1 = 6
6 + 1 = 7
7 + 1 = 8
Merlin needs to make
2 more trips.

Page 9
13 + 1 = 14
10 + 1 = 11
25 + 1 = 26
31 + 1 = 32
3 + 1 = 4
59 + 1 = 60
99 + 1 = 100
199 + 1 = 200
222 + 1 = 223

Page 10
4 + 3 = 7
0 + 2 = 2
4 + 4 = 8
8 + 4 = 12
5 + 1 = 6

Merlin has 8 brothers and
8 sisters. That's 16 in total.

Page 11
6 + 4 = 10
10 + 6 = 16
16 + 3 = 19
5 + 0 = 5
21 + 9 = 30
52 + 2 = 54
48 + 2 = 50

5 + 53 = 58
1 + 101 = 102
8 + 35 = 43

Page 12
Merlin is playing with
8 brothers.
He has 7 lumps of cheese.
PRODUCT does not mean
add (it means multiply).

Page 13
Merlin will be 6.
Mudge has won with
12 points. Merlin has 9.

Page 14
33 - 5 = 28

Page 16
8 - 1 = 7
7 - 1 = 6

6 - 1 = 5
5 - 1 = 4
4 - 1 = 3
3 - 1 = 2
2 - 1 = 1
Kit will have none (0)!

Page 17
11 - 1 = 10
20 - 1 = 19
24 - 1 = 23
13 - 1 = 12
21 - 1 = 20
32 - 1 = 31
1 - 1 = 0
100 - 1 = 99
101 - 1 = 100

Page 18
4 - 1 = 3
6 - 2 = 4
10 - 5 = 5
8 - 4 = 4
9 - 6 = 3

10 - 3 = 7
4 - 3 = 1

Page 19
9 - 2 = 7
10 - 8 = 2
26 - 5 = 21
8 - 7 = 1
32 - 3 = 29

68 - 9 = 59
22 - 2 = 20
13 - 5 = 8
80 - 7 = 73

Page 20
2 birds are left.
Claudius has 4 toys.
If you take 5 from 6 you
get 1.
INCREASE does not mean
subtract (it means add).

Page 21
12 muddy footprints
are left.
Kit has 7 lives.
Claudius has 5.
9 decreased by 3 is 6.
If you subtract 1 from 6
you get 5.

Page 22
11 + 3 = 14
90 - 2 = 88
5 + 5 = 10
18 + 8 = 26
3 - 3 = 0

Whiz-Bang will be
holding 1 wand.
He will have
15 potions.

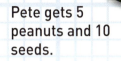

ANSWERS

Page 23
Merlin has 5 berries left.
$10 - 3 - 2 = 5$
Merlin needs to find
13 more.
There will be 17 with 3
steps and 21 with 7 steps.

Page 25
$9 + 1 = 10$
$3 + 7 = 10$
$5 + 5 = 10$
$6 + 4 = 10$
$8 + 2 = 10$

Page 26

Page 27
$7 + 3 = 10$
$5 + 5 = 10$
$2 + 8 = 10$
$9 + 1 = 10$
$7 + 3 = 10$
$5 + 5 = 10$
$1 + 9 = 10$
$6 + 4 = 10$
$6 + 4 = 10$
$8 + 2 = 10$

Page 28
$10 - 8 = 2$
$10 - 4 = 6$
$10 - 3 = 7$
$10 - 5 = 5$
$10 - 9 = 1$

Page 29
$10 - 2 = 8$
$10 - 5 = 5$
$10 - 3 = 7$
$10 - 8 = 2$
$10 - 7 = 3$
$10 - 9 = 1$
$10 - 8 = 2$
$10 - 4 = 6$
$10 - 5 = 5$
$10 - 1 = 9$

Page 30
Blacktooth has 12 tens.
A 5 is left over.
He needs 4 cannon balls.
He has 7 left.

Page 31

$6 + 4$
$9 + 1$
$7 + 3$

$10kg - 3kg = 7kg$
$10kg - 2kg = 8kg$
$10kg - 1kg = 9kg$

Page 33
$5 + 6 = 11$
$5 + 4 = 9$

Page 34
$20 = 10 + 10$
$12 = 6 + 6$
$10 = 5 + 5$
$6 = 3 + 3$
$16 = 8 + 8$

$8 = 4 + 4$
$14 = 7 + 7$
$2 = 1 + 1$
$18 = 9 + 9$

Page 35
$6 - 4 = 2$

Page 36
$8 + 8 = 16$
$8 + 7 = 15$
$10 + 10 = 20$
$10 + 11 = 21$
$3 + 3 = 6$
$3 + 4 = 7$
$5 + 5 = 10$
$6 + 5 = 11$
$7 + 7 = 14$
$6 + 7 = 13$

Page 37
$12 = 6 + 6$
$13 = 6 + 7$
$2 = 1 + 1$
$3 = 1 + 2$
$4 = 2 + 2$
$5 = 2 + 3$
$10 = 5 + 5$
$9 = 5 + 4$
$8 = 4 + 4$
$7 = 4 + 3$
$80 = 40 + 40$
$70 = 40 + 30$

Page 38
The ship's cat is 12.
The other parrots were 8
gold coins.
It takes 16 seconds to fly
there and back.

Page 39
$9 + 10 = 19$
The pizza has 6 slices.

Pete gets 5
peanuts and 10
seeds.

Page 40
$10 - 2 = 8$
$4 + 6 = 10$
$3 + 7 = 10$
$10 - 1 = 9$
$10 - 5 = 5$

1 and 8 do not add up
to 10.

Page 41
Blacktooth is left with
10 diamonds, 9 rubies, 4
sapphires and 7 emeralds.
It takes Pete 6 hours.
$11 + 10 = 21$

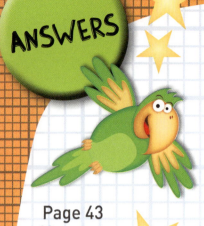

ANSWERS

Page 43

28
45
56

Page 44

23 + 10 = 33
42 + 10 = 52
10 + 57 = 67
10 + 51 = 61
64 + 10 = 74
43 + 10 = 53

Page 45

67 - 10 = 57
18 - 10 = 8
21 - 10 = 11
33 - 10 = 23
49 - 10 = 39
82 - 10 = 72

Page 46

Bella has 45 petals.
The sum of 20 and 10 is 30.
56 is five tens and six units.
Bertie stays for 17 days.

Page 47

There are 43 bugs in total.
There would be 33 left.
There would be 23 left.
They would buy 20 lollipops.

Page 48

The missing totals are
30
50
70
90

Page 49

110 + 90 = 200

Page 50

110 + 50 = 160
200 + 200 = 400
110 + 10 = 120
160 + 30 = 190
210 + 70 = 280
120 + 60 = 180
300 + 40 = 340
190 + 20 = 210

Page 51

120 - 20 = 100
650 - 200 = 450
270 - 50 = 220
150 - 40 = 110
340 - 30 = 310
20 - 20 = 0
330 - 110 = 220

Page 52

The farmer has
10 eggs left.
He has 5 boxes containing 50 eggs.
He has 30 eggs left.
Three tens and three tens make 60.

350 is three hundreds and five tens.
80 + 100 + 10 = 190
70 - 30 is different.

Page 55

6 + 13 doesn't add up to 20.

Page 56

17 + 3 = 20
16 + 4 = 20
1 + 19 = 20
5 + 15 = 20
18 + 2 = 20
22 + 8 = 30

Page 57

20 - 6 = 14
20 - 7 = 13
20 - 9 = 11
20 - 8 = 12
20 - 10 = 10
11 and 8 do not add up to 20.

Page 59

The answer is 3.

Page 60

The differences are 4 and 6.
2 more blue fish are needed.

Page 61

4 pairs have a difference of 5.
The sequences end in
11 (a difference of 2)
1 (a difference of 3)
21 (the differences go up 1, 2, 3, 4, 5)

The difference between
14 and 17 is 3
18 and 6 is 12
2 and 9 is 7.

Page 62

Sid's dad is 2 metres longer.
Sid has 8 more teeth.
B needs 4.
C needs 5.

Page 63

There are 19 dolphins.
The new difference is 3.
He swims the second 200 metres 5 seconds slower.
The sequence ends in 35 (the differences are 1, 2, 3, 4, 5).

Page 64

The difference between the bottles is 5.
30kg will balance the scales.
Hattie has laid 3 more.

Page 65

90 laps in total.
41 and 8 would end in 9.

Page 66
11 + 13 = 24

Page 67
29 + 19 = 48

Page 68
24 + 15 = 39
82 + 16 = 98
18 + 11 = 29
23 + 23 = 46
31 + 24 = 55
55 + 14 = 69
57 + 22 = 79
21 + 42 = 63
66 + 33 = 99
79 + 11 = 90

Page 69
29 + 29 = 58
39 + 19 = 58
49 + 39 = 88
109 + 29 = 138
59 + 19 = 78
19 + 69 = 88
79 + 19 = 98
49 + 49 = 98
29 + 49 = 78
19 + 18 = 37

Page 70
26 - 15 = 11

Page 71
90 - 19 = 71
90 - 21 = 69

Page 72
36 - 25 = 11
28 - 11 = 17
67 - 31 = 36
32 - 12 = 20

54 - 22 = 32
97 - 86 = 11
79 - 52 = 27
21 - 10 = 11
44 - 13 = 31
85 - 23 = 62
101 - 91 = 10

Page 73
70 - 19 = 51
60 - 29 = 31
30 - 19 = 11
100 - 89 = 11
80 - 21 = 59
50 - 31 = 19
40 - 11 = 29
100 - 11 = 89

Page 75
92 - 75 = 5 + 10 + 2 = 17
81 - 38 = 2 + 40 + 1 = 43
74 - 57 = 3 + 10 + 4 = 17

Page 76
69 sips in total.
Georgie runs 11 kph faster.
Georgie eats 35 less in summer.

Page 77
There are 21 males.
There are 25 young ones.
There are 50 adults.
The elephants are beating the zebras by 24 points.
They are beating the giraffes by 36 points.
Yes, they are beating both teams put together.

Page 79

299

746

Page 80

857

787

653 +
33 +
12 =
698

Page 81

356

317 +
60 +
2 =
379

466 +
12 +
1 =
479

555 +
31 +
100 =
686

805 +
23 +
20 =
848

ANSWERS

Page 82
$65 + 12 = 77$
$72 - 61 = 11$
$70 + 22 = 92$
$55 + 25 = 80$
$87 - 64 = 23$
$33 + 33 = 66$

$69 + 69 = 138$
$59 + 49 = 108$
$109 + 29 = 138$

$30 - 21 = 9$
$90 - 39 = 51$
$100 - 51 = 49$
They have 99 feathers.

Page 83
$62 - 47 = 3 + 10 + 2 = 15$

$$\begin{array}{r} 207 + \\ 602 + \\ 80 = \\ \hline 889 \end{array}$$

554

Page 85
$50p - 40p = 10p$
$15p + 15p + 25p = 55p$ The change is 5p.

Page 87

2 COOL CONE 30p
2 CHOC CONE 40p
1 CHOC TUB 25p
1 T-BONE 25p

TOTAL £1.20
CHANGE 30p

1 T-BONE 25p
1 CHOC TUB 25p

TOTAL 50p
CHANGE 50p

You could buy 6 ice creams.

Page 88
40p
£1.10
Option 1 - 5p change
Option 2 - no change

Page 89
75p
25p
Total £4.00
He has £1.10 left.

Page 90
$3 + 6 = 9$ $9 + 2 = 11$ $10 + 7 = 17$ $5 + 5 = 10$

TIMES has nothing to do with subtraction.

Half of 20 is 10.   Double 8 is 16.

$60 - 20 = 40$ $20 + 10 = 30$ $10 + 35 = 45$

The difference between 10 and 15 is 5.

Page 91
$78 + 11 = 89$
$100 - 80 = 20$
$68 + 2 = 70$
$65 - 35 = 30$
$92 - 71 = 21$
$44 - 13 = 31$

You can buy 3 ice creams
with 15p change.

All 4 pairs have a difference of 8.

$$\begin{array}{r} 240 + \\ 34 + \\ 202 = \\ \hline 476 \end{array}$$

$103 - 77 = 3 + 20 + 3 = 26$